LOVE
IS A
HUNGER

Other Books by Earnest Larsen

Liguori Press
Good Old Plastic Jesus
Don't Just Stand There
Where and How
And Tomorrow We
Hey I Love You
Will Religion Make Sense to Your Child
Will Morality Make Sense to Your Child
Not My Kid
You Try Love I'll Try Ajax
Why Don't You Listen
For Men Only
How Do I Change My Man
Depression and Prayer
Spiritual Renewal Of The American Parish I
Spiritual Renewal Of The American Parish II
Spiritual Renewal Of The American Parish III

Paulist Press
Something Wonderful Is Happening
Holiness
Week of Fire

Ave Maria
Godseekers

St. Mary's Press
Busy Being Born

Alba House
Gate of Power
Body of Christ
W.C. Brown
What Ever Happened to Good Old Plastic Jesus

LOVE
IS A
HUNGER

Earnest Larsen

Published by

CompCare
publications

Minneapolis, Minnesota
A division of Comprehensive Care Corporation

(Ask for our catalog, 800/328-3330, toll free outside Minnesota
or 612/559-4800, Minnesota residents)

LC 79-53701
ISBN 0-89638-037-8

4	5	6	7	8
86	87	88	89	90

To Freddie

Contents

This book is a thanks
to the chemical dependency unit
at Mercy Hospital, Anoka, Minnesota,
because a great deal of it
came out of my involvement
with the patients and their families.

LOVE
IS A
HUNGER

Illustrations by Ken Wagner

Love is a Hunger

Love—
for sanity,
for growth,
for our own and others'
safety—
is not a luxury
but an absolute necessity.

Our planet is a huge,
aching,
pain-filled cry for love
and loving;
for being found
and finding;
for reconciliation and rebirth.
Love is not a luxury, something just as well
done without.
Loving to humankind is like
the heart beating,
the mind thinking,
the imagination creating
exciting forms of beauty
on the inner canvas
of the brain.

Love
is at the very center
of who we are
and how we are doing.
Love is necessary.
And—as it is
with all necessities—
when love is denied long enough,
disaster follows,
the world collapses.
A primary objective of psychiatric healing—
and often medical as well—
is to lead the patient
along the difficult but wonderful path
of learning or relearning the skills
of loving relationships.
Every counseling session—
either private or group—
is a step along the line to learned love.

Bill and Jackie,
as hundreds of thousands of other couples,
sit in their counselor's office.
Their marriage has turned sour.
Automatically they say,
"Sure, we love each other but—"
But there is no trust, no kindness.
Their words are poisoned arrows,
their attitude is "attack/defend."
With the counselor's help, they will be led
to a point of decision—
a deciding whether to begin

to try to love
or not.
To learn or relearn some of the skills of
living together in love.
If not—
if these
cannot be learned—
if love is not born between them,
if insights are not gained—
they simply
won't make it.
The seed will have fallen on stone,
and as all seed
fallen upon stone,
it will wither from lack of nourishment.

Dr. Glasser in his works—
—primarily **Reality Therapy**—
says this spiritual nourishment
cannot exist without what he calls
"involvement."
Viktor Frankl in his
Logotherapy calls it
"participation."
Dr. Rollo May in his classic works calls it
"community."
All these are words for
the skills and reality of
shared existence,
of dwelling together in harmony,
of discovering beauty in and
between ourselves and
others.

Erich Fromm in **The Art of Loving**
simply states that
without loving relationships there can be
no love.
Without love there can be
no health.
Without health there can be
only destruction.
St. John calls this necessity
of human living
love,
and Jesus plainly calls it
the greatest commandment.
Though
in our everyday lives we
all too often
treat love or a
loving relationship as a
luxury,
a dimension we can get along without,
in reality
we cannot;
we either love
or we die.
And though there is but one
way to live,
there are a thousand ways to die.

Pat has not yet seen his
twentieth birthday.
Soon he will face the judge for
dealing dope—

narcotics.
Pat
refuses to accept
acceptance.
Those who love him
open their doors wide;
Pat has refused to enter.
Unbroken by love,
he demands to go it alone,
to use others,
to make nothing count but himself.
He has never learned the skills of loving.

Joyce is fourteen.
Somehow,
in whatever way it happens,
she has crossed over the line into
negative-approval-collecting.
The only way she functions is
to make herself unacceptable.
She sulks,
tells everyone how bad she is,
refuses to be happy,
thrives on discord and misery.
As of now
she is cemented in
negative living.
A huge shell has built up around her.
We can only hope,
desperately,
that it may crack open,
as one of our own fights for survival.

When and if it does—
if the shell disintegrates,
it will be love,
the gentle,
relentless,
stronger-than-violence
power of love
that will have made
the difference.
So far,
Joyce knows nothing of love.
She is untouched by its
creative power.

Firm, gentle hand—
or fist of steel?
Acts of caring—
or acts of violence?
The difference
is all a matter of love.

Sometime during that tragic struggle
in Viet Nam,
somewhere in the Ninh Province,
VC prisoners
are huddled together.
Their eyes show
constant fear.
They seem so small,
so young,
so defenseless there,
eyes covered,

hands tied.
A thin American walks up to them.
A strange light burns
within him—
A cruelty,
a hunger,
a demon.
His name
tells it all—
they call him
"Killer."
Silently he waits.
Eyes turn toward him.
His fellow soldiers watch.

He raises his rifle.
Bones and blood fly
in all directions.
Killer
is famous;
he has murdered countless VCs.
In that insane time—
insanity seemed to be
the only measure of normalcy.
A month later Killer himself
is dying.
He lies in the arms of a young medic.
A new kind of light now burns in him;
the cruelty is gone.
His demon wears a different mask.
He tells the medic,
"I never wanted to kill,
never wanted to hurt anyone.
It was only that I could do it well—
the only thing I ever did that people said
I was good at.
They made me feel like a hero.
I wanted so much to be special
to someone. . ."

Love
is not a luxury.
In many different contexts,
we say that love
is the treasure above price
more excellent,
more precious than gold or silver.

We say it, but our lives
at times
betray our lack of belief.
It is love—
not profit,
or being right
or strong or
in control—
that could reduce the number
of those in "psych wards"
and treatment centers—
fill human hearts with the
gentle sweetness
that is a prime ingredient of
sane living.
Our outer world is only an expression
of the mysterious,
powerful,
shadowy world of the inner spirit.
If our world is filled with
anger, hostility, distrust,
then it is so because
the inner worlds
of all too many of us
are starved
and dying—
starved of the harvest of love.

Thank God,
thank Him a million times over
for those people,
those rare, precious, marvelous people

who have learned the secret place
and pitched their tents there.
Those who dwell in the attitudes of
hope and confidence.
Who reach across rather than
down,
those people
whose presence
always leaves us feeling better
about ourselves.
Thank God for these
loving people,
these custodians of the secret of
love.

Phil
is such a custodian.
The treatment center common room
held maybe forty agitated people.
This was the first,
terrifying,
hopeful,
nervous evening of family encounter.
Obviously there was a
disease here,
a killer disease that eroded
trust, faith, and togetherness
like waves washing away a beach.
Eyes darted,
hands twitched.
Excited, meaningless conversation
bounced back and forth.

What would happen?
The hurts had been so deep,
the failures so frequent.
Broken hearts and promises littered the floor
like leaves in the fall.
What would be the cure?
Did someone have a magic answer,
a remedy,
a solution pulled down from the stars
or dredged up from the human heart?
Phil,
the head of the treatment center,
immense in kindness and glowing with
some inner secret,
slowly walked to the front of the room.
He had been here so often,
seen these faces,
felt the desperation,
knew the heartbreak.
The restlessness ceased.
The twitching stopped.
All eyes fixed on his face.
The expectation was ponderous.
"We all have one hope,"
Phil said.
"None of us can get well until we
learn to love.
That is what treatment is all about—
learning to love."

He does indeed
know a secret.

The Fountain

The human spirit can be likened to
a fountain.
The water filling the fountain is
love.
Notice,
when things start going badly,
when fights increase,
when walls begin to rise
obscuring the light of
serenity,
when cruelty bristles—
very probably it is a time when the
fountain is dry.

Love is not a single thing.
It is made of many ingredients.
Those ingredients
fill the fountain.
When a spouse begins to feel like a
servant
or merely one who brings home the pay check,
when the people in a
supposedly loving relationship feel
taken for granted,

gentle attentiveness ceases and
trust evaporates,
when priorities shift to other concerns,
then the fountain becomes bone dry.
Then we had better beware:
A time bomb starts ticking.
Slowly
the members of this relationship begin to feel
alienated
cheated, alone—
waiflike.

The daily tasks—
even vacations that used to be such fun—
these times of togetherness
become chores.
They find excuses not to be
together.
In some strange, unnamed way, there is relief
when something comes up
that allows separateness.
The bomb ticks louder.
In many subtle ways, each of these
"waifs"
makes his or her presence felt—
painfully felt.
Drinking no sweetness from the
fountain,
each has none to give the other.
We learn to punish one another in such
covert ways.
Meals not prepared—
or gotten home to—
topics talked about,
topics avoided,
items bought defiantly,
without consultation—
Then what is covert becomes
overt.
When it is bad enough,
when enough pain has been dealt out
and received,
help is sought—
help to learn and

relearn the skills of love,
the attitudes of love.
It is not a matter of indifference or
secondary importance that the
fountain is dry;
nothing matters more.

The inner need for love and
loving,
for self-worth and participation
in something more
than self is indeed
a hunger.
As with physical hunger,
it cannot be denied.
No one is surprised when
we concede that
one who is starving
will eat almost anything.
Anything!
Given enough hunger, the most
delicate
will fight for scraps.
Hunger turned to starvation
will make anyone
capable of such extremes.

Spiritual hunger is no different.
Endlessly, it seems
the lines of demoralized, disheartened people
pass through offices of all kinds,
seeking help,

drinking gallons of coffee
mixed with tears,
decrying what they are doing,
what is happening to them,
what they have fallen into.
They seem so surprised,
so shocked by what they have done.
Yet
a brief checking into the condition of the
fountain,
the depth of the waiflike feelings,
the unrelieved ticking of the bomb
quickly reveals a tremendous level of
love starvation.
They, too, are fighting for
discarded scraps
because they are so hungry.
It is not a crime to be starving.
It is only a tragedy to consume poisoned food
when something so much more nourishing
is at hand—
or could be.
The main point here, however,
is simply to invite
a measure of the
level of the fountain.
If we consider love a luxury
and do not pursue its
presence in our lives,
do not actively invite it,
put ourselves in the path of love,
then like a bomb, our tensions tick away

and explode,
explode in ways that
destroy our sanity, our
growth and very health.
Certainly,
there is the option to attempt
substitutes.
Facing the dry fountain,
choosing not to deal with it,
we can throw substitutes between
the grinding wheels of life.
Some of us stay busy—
insanely busy;
there are more than a few workaholics around.
If one keeps busy enough, there is no need,
no time or energy,
to work on loving relationships.
As young Joyce did, we can substitute
negative action—
anything to be noticed.
Some may substitute a neurotic form of
religion,
one that takes them so far out of this world
they never have to bother with it,
as if they did not live on planet earth,
crowded together with the rest of us.
Toys
can become a form of attempted escape.
If only, we seem to say,
I can get this other boat, new car or
several new dresses,
then maybe I shall be happy,

this gnawing hunger will vanish,
this aching, empty fountain will
finally be filled.
But there is no substitute for love
but love.

La Mancha.

At one point in that
brilliant play,
Man of La Mancha,
the visionary/hero is confronted by a
"realist."
But the hero,
Don Quixote,
chooses to live with a vision—
a hope of what can be—
to see the good that is around him.

His antagonist accuses him of
not seeing reality,
not seeing life as it is.
Quixote responds
with a question,
what **is** life as it is?
He has seen filthy bundles of humanity
whimpering in the streets,
men killed in war,
poverty and starvation.
Those elements are part of life.
But there is more to life than that.
We choose the world that will be ours.
If we choose to accept

and live in a loveless world,
then that becomes
"life as it is"
for us.
It is never a matter of indifference.
If that becomes our choice,
then the fountains drain dry,
the waifs emerge from the far recesses of our
spirit,
bombs explode.
We teach those around us,
especially the children,
that this is "life as it is."
Expect nothing better.
But it is so
only for those who,
lacking insight and skill,
allow it to be so.

Love as a Relationship

In speaking of the crucial,
vital dimension of human life,
love,
it is important to use
accurate words and concepts.
We often speak of
"**having** love" or
"**being in** love."
This can lead to great confusion,
even to harm.
Love is the name of a relationship.
It is something that happens

between.
These images—
the fountain, the waif and the time bomb—
simply can't be understood
except in the context of **relationship**.
Perhaps another metaphor can be of service.

Most people, at some time or another,
have enjoyed a circus.
Most at least have seen circus acts on television.
We know what a tightrope is.
A tightrope is a line stretched
between
two poles.
There can be no strong line,
no sturdy rope if
both poles are not
capable of holding it up.
There cannot be a one-poled
tightrope.

Love is—
in that sense—
like a tightrope.
It is a relationship stretched between,
flowing between,
existing between
two poles,
two people.
It cannot be stronger,
more true, more creative
than both are willing to make it

and capable of making it.
One person cannot take the full responsibility
for a relationship.
One person simply does not have that kind
of power.
If one pole,
no matter how strong it seems to stand,
is in a relationship with a facing pole
that falters and falls,
then
there can be no creative relationship.
If a rope is
hooked to a fallen pole—
no matter how strong
the other support may be—
it must lie flat on the earth.
Dr. Martin Buber says it beautifully,
". . . feelings dwell in man;
but man dwells in his love.
That is no metaphor but
the actual truth.
Love
does not cling to the I
in such a way as to have the Thou
only for its object, its content
but love is between I and Thou...
Love is
responsibility of an I for a Thou."

One cannot be too
realistic
when looking at the relationship of love,

realistic both in the sense of where it
can go
(and there really is no limit)
and also of where it is,
of what it is.
Fromm specifically called his book
The Art of Loving
because loving is an art.
An art that must be worked at.

And to achieve a loving relationship,
both must work at it.
A tightrope can exist only between
two poles.
One can invite,
hope,
refuse to enable unloving behavior,
but one person cannot take
responsibility for the other,
for the response of the other.
Exactly at this point
is the gross risk of unfairness
in loving relationships.
One
may be both willing and immensely capable
of a loving relationship,
hungering for it,
begging for it,
but if the other person is either unwilling
or unable
to be the opposite end of the relationship,
then
there can be none.
Only increased misery
flows from carrying around an
unreasonable and mistaken
burden of guilt if the primary relationships of
your life are bone dry
and you insist
(or get conned into thinking)
it is all your fault.
As long as the mysterious

powerful flame
or spark
of love still burns
it is imperative to
try,
to invite,
to do all you can to break through the
occlusions that prevent love from flowing,
that keep the rope from stretching
tight.
But that is all one can do—
invite.
One person does not have the power
to march inside the other,
open the doors,
heal the sickness,
let in the sun.
It is not only folly but
dangerous
to think otherwise.
To be mistaken about the nature of love,
about love
as a relationship,
allows anger, hatred, guilt, and the total loss
of self-esteem.

Perhaps this point
can be made clearer.
Let us draw a three-columned page.
On one side is the "I."
In the middle are some of the qualities,
the ingredients,

that go to make up the
jigsaw puzzle of love.
In the third column is the "thou,"
the other.
It would look like this:

I   **THOU**

_____   Trust   _____

_____   Honesty   _____

_____   Emotional Responsibility   _____

_____   Communication   _____

_____   A Sense of Freedom   _____

Just as an indication,
a check list—
Mark the percentages you feel
each of you—
first the "I"
and then the "Thou"—
is contributing to the relationship
in each category.
You may see these percentages,
at least by your estimation,
as vastly different.
They very well may **be**
vastly different.
And that is just the point.

As true,
as achingly true,
as it is that you can only work on yourself,
take the responsibility for yourself,
it is also true
that a loving relationship cannot exist
except to the degree
that both are holding fast to the rope.
To understand that
is to gain freedom
from guilt and false expectations,
if the fountain is indeed dry or drying.
It gives one a much
clearer picture of the nature
of love.
It indicates much more clearly
the options available
and the road to be taken.

As much as love is
a hunger and a skill
as much as it is a relationship,
it is also a process.
There is no such thing as a
static relationship.
If it is not undergoing constant rebirth
and growth,
it is in the act of dying.

Love
is always on the way.
Where it is going is far more
important
than where it is at this moment.
It is the process that counts,
not just the moment.
If a pole or
both poles
in a loving relationship have fallen
but are in the process of being rebuilt,
if both persons
are relearning to trust and care,
then
no matter how long it takes,
it is tolerable.
For by and by
they will "get there"—
only to learn there is no such thing as
a final "there."
"There" is only "better and better."

But if the process is slipping away,
going apart,
then there should be great concern.
For just as there is only
"better and better"
in a process that is traveling love's
precarious path,
there is only
"worse and worse"
for a process going toward separateness.

What direction is it going?
What are the percentages?
What are the elements of the
puzzle
called love?
We so easily say,
"yes, we love one another
but. . . "
But there is no trust, no honesty, no respect,
no kindness.
There is no specialness or attempt to
make the other feel special.
Then how can there be love?
Where is its lovely face seen?
When is its healing touch
felt?
Love
is not a simple, single thing,
but a whole
maze of many elements,
elements upon which the
human spirit feeds
and must sustain itself;
Without these elements,
time bombs explode and
"bundles of filth" whimper in the
street.

With the one we supposedly share a loving
relationship,
we know we should
feel safe—
but such is not always the case.
Many obstacles block the way,
people are taken for granted,
efforts to identify and correct faults cease,
self-centeredness sets in.
Vulnerability is never risked or even
thought of.
Allowing love to **make us**
diminishes to
making love which
degenerates to
routine sex
which becomes a mere functio
What has happened to trust?
Where is it?

There is only one way
a feeling of certitude comes about–
by something
being repeatedly proven.
We have certitude about the sun rising
after it has disappeared
in a beautiful sunset
because it has always come back.
We have experienced it happening.
We can validate it personally.
The only way we can be certain of
trust

Trust

Trust is
the certitude that
the other person
not only will not
hurt me
but is actively involved in the
invitation of my growth.

There certainly can be no
loving relationship,
no tightrope,
without trust.
Obviously trust can mean
many things, can
apply to many levels.
We can speak of trust
as it relates to letting someone use a car
or borrow a dollar.
There are far deeper levels, however,
where trust
relates to more vulnerable
personal dimensions.
But love is a matter of the utmost
vulnerability and

is by others proving themselves
trustworthy.
If that proof,
validated in our lived experience,
is not there,
no matter how much we **want** to trust,
we cannot.
Thus the model of the tightrope;
trust is
not merely a quality we each have separately
but an element
allowed to exist and grow between
two poles.
Trust is
a sharing.

. . . **will not hurt me**

The first dimension of trust—
call it a negative dimension, but it is
essential all the same—
is the certitude the other will not
hurt me.
I know that because
that person has not hurt me thus far.
In a real love relationship,
chances abound
for hurting—
for vulnerability is a piece
of the pie—
but as often as those chances have arisen
there has also been proof of the credibility
that the other,

written in italic letters here
a definition and a
ription.
s a view of an element of love
hat can be tested in the model of the
tightrope.

Trust is first of all a
certainty.
We might say it is a certitude in the
guts rather than the heart,
a feeling rather than a known fact.
They aren't always the sam
Someone we trust
very comfo

the beloved,
will not hurt me.
And that is why I feel safe,
blessedly safe with that person.
Trust
cannot exist in a
win/lose type relationship.
If the process of the relationship
has flowed along the path
that says one has to be right
and, thus,
one wrong;
one has to be smart
and, thus,
one dumb;
one has to be strong
and, thus,
the other weak;
then trust has been murdered.

Often in the company of couples
or "friends,"
if you listen, you may hear the
correction game going strong.
One says it is ten miles to a certain
place—
the other offers a correction, saying
it is ten-and-a-half miles,
to be exact.
One says a lamp costs fifty dollars,
the other says it was fifty-five.
One says the event took place on May 17,

the other says it was May 16.
As a matter of fact, nothing can be said
that is not corrected—
often with tones so sweet
they drip sugar.
The real trouble is on the inside,
in the realm of emotional trust
where there is no sweetness, only
hurt and hiding.

The I
just does not really trust that
the Thou
is supportive.

Just as there is a fine art to
loving,
there is also an art to humor.
Probably as much blood has been spilt
by the mocking joke
as by the sword.
Minimally, trust means
"You won't hurt me."
Yet so often,
in the name of humor,
grave injury is inflicted.

We all have sensitive areas,
such as how we look,
what we have done,
our opinions,
what has befallen us.
In the name of fun
or even friendship,
salt can so easily be rubbed
into those sensitive areas.
It might not be amusing at all
when a wife
jokes about the balding of her
spouse.
No more than when he jokes about
how funny she now looks in her

swim suit.
At a party or gathering, there may be
gales of laughter—
all in fun, of course—
at a recounting of how someone
backed into a fence, ran over a bike,
and dented up the new car.
But it isn't fun.
Embarrassment runs high.
Perhaps one is punishing the other in a subtle,
but oh-so-effective way
about damaging a new toy.
It is not infrequent that
when an embarrassing event has happened,
perhaps even a minor tragedy,
the victim is deathly
afraid
to be around friends,
so low is the trust level.
Losing a pet bird that flew away
through an open cage door
may be a minor event to one
and a catastrophe to another.
For the one to whom it is a catastrophe,
it may cause bitter tears.
Trust vanishes
when those tears are ridiculed.

How often a
"loved one" is
held up to derision,
perhaps under the cover of a joke,

perhaps not,
when one has struck out five times in a
slow-pitched softball game,
had a flat tire and couldn't fix it,
lost a checkbook,
missed a turn in the road on a trip
or forgotten
to bring the sandwiches for a picnic.
No matter
what the ridicule
hides under,
the fact remains:
when love and
sensitivity are lacking,
when these hurting events are dragged out
time after time,
a person can bring about
self-fulfilling prophecies—
you **know**
the other will make fun of you,
and it happens.
But when there is love,
real love,
one never makes the other feel stupid
or inadequate.
Love protects the other.
Trust is that part of love that knows
the protection
will always be there
because
it always has been.
Still, a minimal part of

trust
is the acceptance that
the other at least cares
about what I want.
It is not just a one-sided affair,
in which the other
always decides what will happen,
where we go,
what we buy—
nor is it always a situation in which
"you decide—we'll do whatever you want."
Because you know that isn't true;
it is only a hiding place.
For when **you** decide,
then if anything goes wrong,
or if it is not pleasing to the other,
it's your fault,
you come in for the blame.
These deeper levels of trust
always call into existence the reality of
we.
We decide,
we talk it over,
for we are walking this walk
together.
I trust that you will be there.
I trust you will not only not go alone
but will not
hurt me if
I attempt to come with you.
Rising above the level of minimal trust
is good, but it is not good enough

for a loving relationship.
If the relationship is in the process
of rising above that minimal level—
wonderful!—
it will get there.
But with it must rise
the certitude that one is also being
actively invited to grow.
Love is a journey,
a process,
a growth.
Trust
in love
means not only that I
am walking that journey but
inviting you to journey with me.

The invitation to grow is
always
an invitation to rise above fear.
Fear is the enemy.
It is the
"in spite of" that
Paul Tillich clearly states
stands between ourselves as we are
and as we could be.
In courage, we face the
"in spite ofs"
along our path of life and
strive to do, to be, and
to open up.

Trust—
without which there can be no
loving relationship—
is the felt certainty that the other
is actively involved in
encouraging and helping me over these
obstacles.
This trust certainly can't exist if one is
always afraid of being
hurt by the other.
Fear prohibits us from doing
so many things.
Locked up in many of us is a
wish to write a poem,
to make a table,
to sing a song,
to read a book or
attempt some project we always dreamed of.
Then why don't we?

More often than not the reason is
fear.
Fear of failure,
fear of ridicule
fear of doing it alone.
Trust is believing
(because it **is true**)
that the other will always encourage me to do
what my dreams tell me.
That other rejoices in my
accomplishments,
glories in my growth,

invites
rather than demands,
encourages rather than
cajoles,
smiles rather than
jeers.
If I finally make something on a
potter's wheel
that other proudly displays it in the house;
if I finally join that discussion club,
that person is anxious to go along with me or
to hear what happened.
If I make a good dinner
or hit a home run in a game,
there is cheering,
not laughing.
Trust is making
each other feel good
about ourselves
and what we can do.
People who don't make us feel good
about what we do,
and can do,
we simply don't trust.

A deeper truth is that trust in
what we can **do**
has a profound bearing on
our courage to **be**.
Doing and being
are not the same thing:
nor are they totally separate.

In general the more we discover
we can do,
the more we know who we are.
The more confidence we possess,
the greater the possibility of
a sound, healthy self-image.
In this second dimension of
positive presence—
deeper than trust to **do**—
is the trust to **be**.
Trust on this level is the
loving affirmation of who we are.
There is a great land-locked ocean
in almost everyone,
potential not yet discovered,
not yet dared to be let out.
There are words floating around
that have not found the substance
they fit;
the words are ourselves—
as yet unsung.
Trust is knowing
positively that
the other wants those
oceans to be undammed,
those potentials actualized.
This, of course, can happen in many ways
but not without dialogue.

It is amazing how many people say
"We love each other,
but we never talk."

There can be talk without
dialogue
(because nothing is said),
but there cannot be dialogue without
talking.

Two people I know—
a couple greatly in love—
have a room in their house called the
quiet room.
They have five young children;
their house is a noisy place,
but there is still a quiet room
which exists because it is needed,
just as the kitchen is needed.
And this because love is needed
and there can be no love
without trust,
and there can be no deeper trust
without quiet talking.
In a loving dialogue,
planned and regular,
we slowly learn it is okay to be
who we are.
And, in fact, to go beyond that
and discover
who we can be.
Our others want that.
They want it
because our growth is important
and because the more we are
the more power we have to invite the others
to be all they can be.

The kids slowly go to bed,
the chores are completed,
things are put away—
quiet time.
Vital, essential, quiet time.
Time to listen and to speak,
to reveal and be receptive,
to get in touch with who we are and
where we are going;
to hear our song,
what we have said to one another,
and are saying.

In no other way do we ever come to believe
we are worth knowing,
in no other way do we ever
trust that the other
wants to know who we are
and in return to be known by us.

This level of trust is heady wine.
But so is love.
The third level of trust in this
positive vein,
after trust to **do**
and to **be**,
is the trust to **open up**.
Opening up has to do with
vulnerability.
The more we trust, the more
we are willing to let others know
who we are—
our inner selves.

The deeper the journey, however,
the greater the vulnerability.
The more we trust, the more
distrust
slaughters us.
The more the sacred qualities of
trust in love are present, the more
one can hear,
in all that passes between the lovers,
"Please, let me in."
At first sound it seems confusing—
let you in where?
What do you want?
You **are** in!
Where else is there to go?
But if the journey is genuine, there
never is an end
to the in-ness that is possible,
possible only through
trust.
Trust, then,
such an essential element of love,
is the proved
presence
of one another.
The certainty that I am safe here,
I shall not be hurt.
Far beyond that is the
reciprocal trading of vulnerabilities.
For two people to have trust between them,
however, there must also be
emotional responsibility.

Emotional Responsibility

Emotional responsibility is
**the loving redemptive
response to the
vulnerability of the other**.

The reason there is such a
dearth
of trust in loving relationships
is because there is such a
dearth
of emotional responsibility.
Trust and responsibility
are a resonance.
Neither stands alone in the context of a
relationship—
one is the response to the other.
These is a soft call from the depths,
depths of one
to the depths of another.
At one time the "I"
is giving in trust,
rendering the gift of vulnerability—
at another time it is rendering the gift of
responsibility

listening to,
accepting,
receiving the vulnerability
of the other.
When one vital piece of the puzzle is lacking
the whole puzzle is unfinished.
The conversation has ended.
There cannot be a conversation
unless both persons
are involved.
If neither speaks—
or both speak at the same time—
there is no
space between—
it has been choked off.

The word
"emotional"
has been placed in front of responsibility
for a major reason.
All too often the word
"responsibility"
calls to mind merely physical
responsibility.
Frequently we will hear reasoning like
"She's got a roof over her head.
What else does she want?"
Or
"He has his meals cooked and his
shirts cleaned:
I'm doing my part."
This, of course, indicates

that the relationship is merely
functional,
that people are relating to one another
only on a physical level,
that humans are only
physical beings.
Certainly this is not the case.
Spiritual and emotional responsibility
are far more important.
Obviously you can have deep, abiding
love
in a mud hut—
and the very essence of hell
in a castle.

The two dynamics to consider in
emotional responsibility are the
response
and the invitation.
Response has to do with the place of
vulnerability in love.
The precise response we are talking about
is the response to vulnerability shared in trust.
In all true loving relationships
one doesn't love the
pretense or masks of another person,
but the other person.
The more the one
is able to say and share:
"Hey, this is me,
I don't have to hide or
pretend,"
the more there is to love.
The task therefore is to allow more
of ourselves to be
known.
The process by which we allow that to happen—
our own emergence—
is the process of increasing
vulnerability.
The question in emotional responsibility
is how we respond to that gift.

The subtlety of this is
enormous.
I recall once on a picnic—
a lovely day—

listening to a husband try to
encourage his wife to play volleyball.
He really wanted her involved.
She thought herself most unathletic
and was greatly afraid to attempt the game.
She didn't trust.
Patiently at first he prodded her,
explaining that there really was
nothing to it.
The ball was big and soft.
It floated over toward her and all she had to do
was hit is back.
She was afraid.
Increased prodding produced
increased fear.

It all ended by him shouting,
"Don't be so damn dumb—
all you have to do is stand there and
hit the thing."
Needless to say,
she never did.
I don't know if this couple have a
quiet room.
I don't know if they ever speak to
one another,
if they ever confide hurts and injuries.
If they do, then perhaps they will see that
she was afraid
and force is never a solution to fear.
At first she was ready—
hesitatingly—

to try,
but the louder and more
demanding the response,
the more she tended to hide,
the more fear won.

The woman may never be a good athlete.
It doesn't matter.
With enough emotional responsibility,
the couple can find
much fun
and companionship,
playing many sports.
But she was hurt,
that part of her "I"
which was vulnerable on the volleyball court
receded further into the background,
perhaps never to come forward again.
There is less of her
"I" to love—
she will not allow herself to be seen.

We can be afraid of so many things,
hide so much.
Some people are afraid of darkness.
For others this makes no sense.
If the one
trying to deal with this fear
verbalizes it
and is met with something like
"Well, that's the dumbest thing I ever heard,"
the attempt probably will end.

Responsibility, like a broken bridge, had failed.
I know a young man who is terribly frightened
of heights.
One summer working on a construction gang
he was given the job of carrying out
small buckets of cement to a swinging scaffold
thirteen floors above the ground.
The scaffold could be pushed out
from the face of the wall,
leaving only air under him
for thirteen floors down.
It became a great sport when
trembling,
faltering,
terrified,
he inched his way onto that scaffold,
for the men
to push the apparatus out,
letting it slam back against the building.
Such senseless cruelty passed as
routine
with this gang.
What is not so obvious is that all too often
similar cruelty passes as
routine
in our primary and secondary relationships.
We simply cannot be trusting for long
in the face of one who is not
responsible.

The flip side of
emotional responsibility is

invitation.
As it is **not** true that we are
responsible for the decisions of another,
not responsible for that person's growth
or decisions,
it is true that
we **are** responsible for the invitation.
An invitation is not a demand.
A demand states
that there had better be a response
and an appropriate one,
or there will be punishment.
An invitation truly says
"I would like your company.
I ask for it.
If you elect not to come
that is your choice.
I will not punish you for
your way,
it is yours to choose."
Another way of saying this would be:
We are not responsible for the door opening,
but we are responsible for a gift being there,
if and when the door is opened.

The practical application
or at least the question this raises in
relationships is—
if we have a complaint that our others
can't love,
perhaps we should take a deeper look at
whether or not

they have been invited to love.
If they seem so very uncreative and
ordinary,
perhaps they have not been invited to be
any different.
To such a surprising degree
we are very much
what we have been invited to be.
In the process of straightening out
marriage problems
or any relational problems,
it is a vastly different thing to sit back
demanding that the other change
than it is to be
actively involved in the
invitation
for the other to change,
to grow.
One attitude sees the model of
a loving relationship
as unipolar.
It says
"When **you** change,
then the rope will be stretched tight."
The other recognizes the
true nature of relationships in general
and loving relationships in particular.
There is no such thing as one pole
not affecting the other
and the rope between them.
For one person to change—
if the relationship is to continue—

there must be the invitation from the other.
Lacking this,
there may well be a change,
but the invitation will come
from some other source.
The response to healing and growth then
will be to the source
from which it came.
Whatever the source,
that will become the emotional center of the
other's life.
The call then
from deep unto deep
will be from that person to the other.
One relationship will die;
another will be born.

What is absolutely astounding in this
often repeated phenomenon is that
the very qualities
found so lacking in one relationship
are the same ones predominant
in another.
What has been born is not so much
something that was never there
as the qualities invited to emerge
by a loving, concerned other.

"We love each other,
oh, sure, we love each other—
but. . ."
But we never talk,

58

never invite,
never truly trust one another.
And slowly the
eagle that is in each one begins to fly
in another sky.
When that happens for a long enough time,
there no longer is
anything in common.
The relationship has ended.

Just to see that love is a
relationship and that
all relationships are in process,
going somewhere,
is a healing in itself.
It is a hope in itself.
The emotional responsibility—
both to respond to the vulnerability
of the other
in a loving, redemptive way
and
to invite the other
to come out of hiding—
is essential in the growing process of
love.

However,
the eye both of
trust and emotional responsibility
is honesty.

Honesty

Honesty is
**the conscious effort to eliminate
games from my life
and therefore from the relationships
in which I am involved**.

Honesty
like trust
admits of different levels.
We can speak of honesty as
not lying to one another,
giving back change
when we have been overpaid,
returning a lost wallet.
It is a far different matter, however,
to be involved in the
conscious pursuit of our dishonest games.
There we are
speaking not of
honesty with others
but with ourselves.

Self-honesty is the willingness,
fearlessly,
to **look**.
Without looking we really don't
see, .
and without seeing we are
truly blind.
Without honesty, we genuinely can't know
or even guess,
it we have been or are
trustworthy,
if we have been or are
emotionally responsible.
We don't know where we are—
or where the other is—
in the relationship of love.
It gets all blurred,
confused,
mixed up.
We don't know if we are dealing with
our own games or others'.

Love is a relationship between an I
and a Thou.
Person to person.
Facing one another.
Games fuzz up what is going on.
Games stand like
dirty windows
between the light of truth
and who I really am,
what I am doing,

62

who the other is,
what that person is.
Dirty windows not only
prohibit the light of truth from coming in,
they also keep us
from seeing out.

Hide the hatchet
is a favorite game.
What that means is—
there has been a hurt,
a misunderstanding,
perhaps an instance of cruelty.
The tightrope was not taut, the
relationship was not healthy enough
to talk it through.
There was not enough trust or responsibility—
so the hatchet
was hidden.
(But not hidden too deep,
for it must be at hand.)
A week or a month down the road
something comes up—
Out comes the hatchet.
Blood spills in bucketfuls.
The hatchet-swinging has nothing,
nothing to do with the moment.
It is left over from the past injury—
still unhealed.
What can then happen
is that the injured person tries to deal
with the symptom.

But the symptom is not the
cause.
The cause took place months—or years—ago.
What is being dealt with
is **not** the issue.
So nothing is healed.
It is a deadly game.

If the game-playing runs deep enough,
is severe enough,
there is not even the desire to name
what is really going on.
That, too,
is part of the game.
Not naming the problem makes it
unhealable.
You can never get to it.
The hatchet goes in the
back pocket again,
awaiting another opportunity
to jump into action.

Honesty is the
conscious pursuit
of the elimination
of such games.

Another game that
frequently
obliterates the possibility of love,
thus
deadening our world, is

"peace at any price."
What this game says is that
communication is too difficult.
I do not want to face
and name a situation that is killing me.
So I deny it.
I say it isn't there.
I buy into the attitude of
"peace at any price."
The result, however, is that there
never is any peace
and
the price is always too high.

One of the price tags—
far too high—
of this game is this:
people, like relationships,
are never static.
People are in motion—
they are becoming.
The more we allow ourselves
to tolerate the intolerable,
the more we sanction and
enable
others to solidify their destructive
behaviors.
Then we are the ones left
to live with those games.
Then we are the ones who must
increasingly
blind our inner eyes

to the destruction around us
in order to survive.
If that situation is not getting
better and better,
then it is getting
worse and worse.

There can be a mysterious line
inside a person,
a demarcation
beyond which there is no
graceful coming back.
Sometimes this is very visible.
The eyes grow hard.
The face never indicates what is
really there underneath.
Hostility replaces softness,
walls replace doors.
It is a tragic transformation to see.
Truth
seems to frighten these people,
as though, if truth were embraced,
some protective shield
would be stripped away
and the exposure would prove fatal.
Once
that line is passed and
negativism sets in,
any remedy will involve both
time and pain.
You can't push or rush these people,
you can't coax or drive them
(though they will take every bribe you offer).
As good as you are to them,
in your best efforts,
they seem to relish hoarding up
hatchets
to chop down the very ones who
love them most.

It all seems so senseless—
the pain, I mean.
Endless hours of
counseling seem
fruitless, for
there seems to be no capacity for honesty,
no truth,
no vision.

Everything said
gets turned around,
twisted somehow.
Alibis and excuses,
often born of true genius, appear.
There are no corners
for these negative ones;
they will not be caught.
Obviously
there is no easy cure
or answer to such a common, tragic situation.
But one thing is sure:
The game of
"peace at any price"
is no answer
or help.
In fact, somewhere along the line
that game—
tolerating the intolerable,
excusing and enabling
irresponsibility—
may have helped form a pattern.

In all Twelve-Step programs they speak of
the elephant in the front room.
Live long enough with that
elephant,
and you don't even know it's there.
You accept it.
Every night while
reading the evening paper or watching the
news on TV,
you haul out the hay and water to
feed the beast—
it becomes part of the family.
A visitor may drop in and be
incredibly shocked.
"My God,"
the caller says,
"You have an elephant in your front room!"
Our response all to often is
"Where?
I don't see an elephant."
We don't even know it's there.

"Guilt"
easily becomes a favorite game.
We seem to be such a
guilt-prone people.
Guilt is
easily used to
keep people in line—
just where we want them.
If our attitude is not one of
promoting their growth

and happiness—
truly **for** them—
then we want them
for **us**.
We don't want so much what is
best for them
but
what is best for us—
what makes us look good
or feel fine,
even if it kills them.
Take food, for instance:
I know a physical fitness buff
who exercises constantly.
He believes
excess pounds are the scourge of the world—
not only his,
but anyone else's as well.
His wife is not fat,
nor
is she a physical fitness buff.
The man loves the way he looks;
he doesn't love the way
she looks.
In his mind
she
makes him look bad.
Guilt becomes his weapon.
He makes her feel horrible if there is a
cookie
around the house.
He asks her what she ate

when she went out with her friends.
Never in an angry,
hostile, accusing way—
but quietly—
with a smirk and sneer.
Tension is like a
killing smog around their house.

He innocently says,
"I want her healthy,
I don't want her to die of a
stroke or something."
He is the good guy,
She the bad.
She says that isn't true.
What he is most concerned with
is how she looks
when she is with him
around his friends.
The obvious point is—
they don't trust one another.
Trust is absent because
responsibility doesn't exist.
Nor can it without
honesty.

Guilt truly can
control people, but
love is not a matter of controls.
If controlling is the goal of
"love,"
as understood by one of the two,

real love can never exist.
If he puts on enough pressure
and she buys into
"peace at any price,"
she may shrink to a shadow.
But there will never be love.
It was demanded—
not invited.
As the fountain dries,
the waif stands out more starkly,
the hunger increases.
The body may have stopped eating,
but the spirit rages on.
A substitute will be found,
something at least to
ease the inner gnawing.
That substitute may well be
poison.
Somewhere along their lives' path a
counselor or doctor may ask them,
"But what went wrong?
What happened?
How did you end up like this?"
And blind eyes may look from
tanned faces in utter
bewilderment.
"I don't know—
I really don't know."

Love is not a luxury;
it is an absolute necessity for
sanity, health, growth
and safety.

Prophets

A prophet's job is
to tell—or foretell
the truth.
Prophets come in all forms.
Each of us needs our own
tellers of truths,
our own prophets.
The trouble is—we often
kill our prophets because
we don't really want to hear the truth.
With healthy attitudes
between us, we can be
prophets to one another.
We can talk to one another.
We can ask for others' visions,
for their perspectives,
their views.

"This is the way it seems to me,
how do you see it?"
It seems so simple,
yet it is not.
For such a question demands that we listen
and **want** to hear.
If we are involved in some game
or other
that is casting ruin around us,
it is vital that we listen
as the others speak.
It is vital that each of us has someone,
that we each allow someone
in our lives that we can
and will ask.
If we do not have
our prophets, who is left to
tell us the truth?

It is not important here to offer
an exhaustive list of games,
dishonest ways we
deal with one another.
The point is that
without honesty
and the desire for honesty,
the conscious pursuit of it,
we don't know the games we are playing.
With our inner window
thus dirtied,
we don't know or recognize the games
being played with us either.

Love,
being a process,
can certainly tolerate slow growth,
the climbing out of dishonesty; but
it cannot tolerate willed dishonesty.
Love
flies on the wings of communication.
Willed dishonesty
breaks the very wings
that would carry us into the heavens.

Communication

Communicating
indicates **passing through
the point of pain
to deeper understanding**.

The sign simply read,
"The only way out is through."
It could have hung anywhere.
This one hung on the wall
of a treatment center.
Its truth is endless.

Frequently
when arriving at a hard place,
a place full of pain,
we don't go through;
we try to go around.
We go around by ignoring the problem,
calling it by another name,
dealing with a symptom,
confronting someone who has
nothing to do with the problem.

Communication
is the act of going through.
And that act is always the result of
a choice.
We choose to want to
communicate or not.
Of course, again—
communication takes two;
it is a decision both make.
But once made,
the mysterious, marvelous, magical
insides
of both the
I and the Thou
are able to know and be known.
Hiding stops.
Energy
that was spent on
running to escape
is now expended on
revelation.
We want to know each other
as we really are
and are becoming,
what is behind the things we do,
what old patterns we wrestle with.
Will we go back to being waifs?

A waif
is one who feels
left out,
used,

not loved;
one who has a feeling
in the pit of the stomach
of what it's like to
stand outside a warm,
lovely
store window
with not a dime to spend,
shoes full of snow.
Feeling like a waif
is a sickness,
a hurt.
It is easily healed, however,
at least temporarily.
To heal the waif,
it takes
a loving arm around the shoulder,
or a sincere
"How are you?
Want to talk?"
A hand held out,
an invitation to join in—
be part of the crowd.
These things are what it takes.
How often have we seen
the lone wolf,
scared, hurt, alienated,
standing alone,
spewing hurt and pain to all around
become absorbed in
a totally different reality
when invited in.

Into love,
into the group,
into involvement with them.
Every conversion story ever told,
every situation
of one ransomed,
redeemed,
is the story of a waif who found
home;
of a yellow-eyed wolf
wandering the back timbers
of consciousness
who finally found a way out,
and in that loving invitation
lost its claws and fangs,
lost its desire to tear and rip,
lost the urge to fight.
Only estranged waifs
deported to the fringes of love
need respond to their world with
anger, violence, and hostility.

Love is not a luxury.

At times all of us feel
the waif in us.
Some,
because of past experiences
or tender personality,
feel it much more than others.
When the waif is in control,
either there is communication

or there is disaster.
Now here is the problem:
For most it is extremely difficult to say,
"I feel so alone,
rejected,
left out."
The reason, of course, is because
of fear,
lack of trust,
lack of responsibility.
It is hard to ask
"Please, love me."
The temptation is to
act out all sorts of other games,
get irritated about the weather,
moan about supper,
complain about the cost of living.
It gets worse and
worse.
But
communication is the word,
the act of passing
through
the point of pain to a deeper,
more genuine understanding
of who we are as individuals and
as poles supporting the tightrope
of a loving relationship.

If we are communicating, one can say,
"The waif is in control,"
trusting, knowing

the other will gently say,
"Let's talk about it."
Perhaps
it was something done,
a single act
or a series of miniscule events that
alone
amount to nothing
but collectively become mountainous.
Very possible it was a misunderstanding,
something wrongly
interpreted.
A look assumed to mean
"You bore me,"
or
"Why don't you stop saying such dumb stuff,"
or
"You sure do silly things."
Did that look **really** say that?
We suppose,
but we don't know.
True,
it is risky and painful to say.
"Is this what you meant?"
It is a crossroads of pain.
Communication
is the act of facing and then
passing through
together,
that crossing, where there is a
stumbling block or stepping stone in the road.

Once friends,
lovers, couples or groups
have faced such crossroads of pain
and passed through,
they can have the surety that it
can be done.
Communication is possible.
On the wing of such surety
trust is born.

Of course the waif feeling
is but one kind of moment,
one point of pain.
There are many.
There can be conflicts over
money management,
time expenditure,
manners,
politics, religion—
a list without end.
There never will or can be
a time in the process of
building a loving relationship when
points of pain are nonexistent.
Love is not free.
The price we pay is our willingness and ability
to pass through those points of pain,
whatever they may be:
we emerge, perhaps scarred,
but deeper and better
for the passage.

There is an alternative—not a happy one—to
communication,
just as there is an alternative to love.
What often is substituted for
genuine communication is fighting.
Fighting becomes
the elephant in the living room,
familiar,
comfortable,
accepted.
When it becomes accepted, however,
again it becomes a self-fulfilling prophecy.
When points of pain emerge
we just know
"we are going to have a fight"—
and we do.
But there are other options,
infinitely preferable to cruel,
demeaning fighting.
Fighting,
with all the verbal abuse that often goes
with it,
as in the case of all violence,
is a proof of failure.
Violence in all its forms
is the expression of powerlessness.
As long as we feel there is power to
handle a situation in some other way,
we do not resort to violence.
Violence is the ultimate failure.
Not only is there all too often
fighting

in lieu of communication,
but often
it is said that fighting is good,
necessary release.
Cruelty is never beneficial.
There are creative ways of dealing with
rising emotions—
anger,
disappointment,
resentment—
but they may well be painful.
If we understand
fighting
to mean the crash, out of control—
the burst of emotion,
often dishonest to the core,
then

there is no good in that.
It is a retreat
that must be made up
if the relationship is to continue.
Supposed lovers
and friends
can become accustomed to fighting.

They glibly say
it is no big deal.
But this should not be said
too quickly.
Trust
is a very nebulous quality,
fragile for all its strengths.
Fighting
often brings out angry,
hostile words and emotions,
and trust is violated.
This is not to say that
friendships don't continue,
that one avoids the company
of the other.
But all too often there is not as much
openness,
not as much invitation.
No one likes to have a
tender spot rubbed
(even if the rubbing
is in the name of a good-natured fight)
or to be subjected to
violent abuse.

The pain is still there.
It still hurts.
And we are less
likely to expose that
tender spot again.

Some have even said it is
good
for kids to see their parents fight.
It gives them a taste of
"reality."
What reality?
It is far better for children
to see adults
encounter points of pain,
potential battlegrounds,
and handle them in a creative,
loving manner,
than it is to witness
violent scenes of disrespect
and injury.
Children are defenseless against their
environment.
If they live with models of
hurt and injury, then these do indeed
become their reality.
What a precious gift
to offer children—
the knowledge that there is a different
reality
than abuse.
found-ness.

Communication
comes from two Latin words,
which, when combined,
mean to build a wall together.
It means pulling side by side—
as partners.
Perhaps more in our age than in any other,
there is a vast, gloomy, hideous
fear of being alone,
isolated and alienated.
The prospect of not having an
other,
of having no one to pull with you,
lies at the root of innumerable
cases of both mental and
physical illness.
We are not made to live in isolation.
Yet
so many of us find ourselves
right there,
alone and un-found.

In communication,
we experience the
exquisite sweetness of being found.
We dared to say,
"This is the real me,"
as though we were saying
a password before a menacing gate,
and the response was
"Enter."
How we hunger for
home,

for a place to belong,
to come into and rest.
How worth the effort not
to end the journey at a point of
pain,
but to pass through—
to reach out a hand,
perhaps into the darkness,
into distrust and doubt,
but reach it out all the same,
asking someone to respond
and
together,
hand in hand,
journey on.
The price is high,
the risk great,
but the reward is greater.

When communication is
sincerely sought
and achieved
—for in sincerely seeking we are
communicating—
we arrive at another most
essential
piece of the puzzle of love.
That is:
We discover for certain that the
others
seek only to set us free,
not to possess us.

A Sense of Freedom

Only those individuals who have chosen
to lean without losing their
individuality can participate in a
loving relationship.

Love
is a necessity, not a luxury.
As with every necessity there is a
"have to"
attached to it.
There is no
"have to"
with a luxury—
that is why whatever it is
is a luxury.
A necessity
at the heart of love
is for both persons,
both poles,
to retain their integrity as individuals.
Individuals are persons who can truly
say "I."
These are my tastes,

opinions,
likes and dislikes—
this is what is negotiable and
this is what is not.
There is an "I" here
who has the power to make choices,
to decide,
an "I" who will listen,
consider,
evaluate,
but then will take the terrifying
risk to say,
"I choose,
I decide."

It is true—
as it has been repeatedly said in these pages—
that love is a
relationship.
It does not reside in one pole
but exists in the space between.
It is true that
for love there must be a pulling together,
a common building;
but there must also be a
distinct "I"
or there is no pole.
It is not within the nature of love
that one pole
of the relationship becomes
or allows itself to become
a mere shadow of the other.

One part cannot become
a blotter
that absorbs anything poured before it.
It is paradoxical,
but not contradictory,
that love demands two,
but each one of those two
must be
at least on the way
to being a true individual.
The rope
stretched between the poles falls
when one person attempts to
own or
dominate the other,

when one must be slave to
the other's master,
one dumb
to the other's smart,
one wrong
to the other's right.
Only free individuals
are capable of
free decision.
Regardless of the risk and
fear,
that springs like some
protective shield in a
science fiction movie
when the thought of
setting someone free emerges,
it must be done.
If I
have to
love you I can't.
No one can love by **having** to.
I can be forced
to render
obedience,
service,
time,
but not love.
So often when the
spark,
the sweetness,
has gone out of a loving relationship
the outer manifestations have not changed;

there still are the same
meals, the same
routines,
the same vacations and parties,
but something vital is missing.
what has died is the
free choice,
the decision,
the **want** to
that can only be when you know,
in trust,
the other wants you to be
the best **you**
you can be.
For that **you**
is the only you there is
to bring into your relationship.
The attitude of love
is not to possess
but to set the other free.

Once free,
a person can then
choose to lean
or to walk alone.
Love is leaning.
It is the choice to lean.
What does it mean
to "lean"?
On one hand to "lean" means
to risk,
to allow ourselves to need each other.

Our world would not be the same
without each other.
That difference
goes far beyond
physical or monetary considerations.
Emotionally
there has been a rooting process
going on,
a coming together,
a melting.
When we lean,
we are as willing,
(if perhaps not always as able)
to share a weakness,
a fault or fear
as we are a strength,
a success or a victory.
Leaning means being willing to
turn oneself inside out
in the presence of the other,
so that all that is beautiful
can be celebrated
and all that is broken can be
tended to.
The attitude of leaning
was tenderly portrayed
in the award-winning movie, **Rocky**.
He had gone the distance,
all fifteen rounds.
In his own way he had won;
he was the champ.
It was his moment in the spotlight.

People pushed and crowded around;
they wanted his attention,
his words, his thoughts and emotions.
But Rocky had learned to
lean
without losing his own identity.
He wasn't nearly so
caught up,
absorbed,
carried away
by all the adulation as he was
desperately looking for his Adrienne.
He wanted her,
to share this moment with her,
to bring her into the spotlight as well.

He didn't want to be there,
glamorous as it was,
alone.
The sweetness of their
coming together
would never have happened if
they had not,
all along,
also shared their fears, their hard times,
their doubts and disappointments.
They had risked
when, in their vulnerability,
each could have been devastated
by the other.
So now they could also share,
by leaning,
the thrilling ecstasy of victory.
On the other hand,
leaning is more
than just risking vulnerability,
asking the other to
be there for you.
It is also the
"summum bonum,"
as Robert Frost called it,
the greatest good
one gives another
in love.

In our production-oriented world,
our efficiency-minded,
perfectionistic,

get-the-job-done
society,
it is extremely difficult
not to be influenced
wholly by these attitudes.
When one of us chooses
to lean, however,
in a loving relationship,
trusting that
the other is asking us to lean as well,
we are not talking about
earning or
production or
job ratings.
What one member
in a loving relationship always says is:
"First of all,
lean;
first of all, need me;
first of all, in our
individuality
let us be One.
Then,
then we can deal with all the rest.
But first of all,
let us lean."

All too often our
response,
if ever we find ourselves in such a
situation, is
much like Tevye's wife's in the play,

Fiddler on the Roof,
when he asked her if she
loved him.
Embarrassed, taken by surprise,
she started to spout
a thousand stammering things
she had done for him,
things they had done together during
a life lived many years side by side.
But
these weren't answers to
Tevye's question.
Those were functional answers to a
spiritual question.
His response was along these lines:
"Yes, I know all those things;
that isn't what I am asking.
What I ask is
do you love me?
Are we more than living
side by side?
Are we also together?
Has the melting wax of our
lives
flowed as one,
making a third
and new reality
that can never be the same if one
departs,
that in fact never can be
taken apart?"
"Side by side" we live

legally;
"together,"
involves the spirit.

The invitation to lean does not,
first of all, say,
"Make a lot of money,
be an expert cook,
never get old,
play with the kids,
be handy with tools,
love to discuss
what I like to talk about."
All of those may well be important
for our loving relationship,
but first of all
something else must be considered:
First of all, let us
lean,
as two cards
supporting and holding one another up.
If one falls,
so does the other—
not in the sense that the individual goes under
but that the relationship is broken.

By leaning—
strange as it may seem—
we set our others free
because it is a recognition of their
worth and importance in our lives.
Leaning

obviously calls for a decision
and a risk.
The decision is about what
is really important;
the risk is that
if one decides the relationship is the
number one priority
and the other doesn't,
there is heartbreak ahead.
And yet the sad fact is:
If the relationship is **not** number one
something else must be.

From time to time, there have been
random polls taken concerning
"the most important thing in your life."
The answers, as you can imagine,
range all the way from having
money or success to saving one's soul.
Each answer, of course, is open to
wide interpretation.
However,
if the relationship,
consisting of both poles and the
"rope" between,
is not of primary importance, then it will
suffer,
possibly collapse.
Would it not be fascinating to give
the persons in any loving relationship
a chance to express
what each would perceive

as the number one priority in the relationship
as well as the number one priority
of the other.

Granted that in such instances
there is often discrepancy between what is
said and what is
lived,
this could offer insight.
Possibly there might be such items on the
list as
golf, hunting, playing cards
or
walking with friends, spending money, church.

How many people,
how often,
would put as first
"helping the other,
the one I love,
to know that he or she is number one in my life,
that our relationship,
our being together,
is most important to me
for
that is what I have chosen."

Without that attitude being present,
there is immense danger
of the dry fountain,
the waif-feeling
the ticking bomb
exploding.

It is our choice about what is
number one to us.
Yet how easy it is to slip into the attitude of
"I can't help it."
It's not my fault the golf league meets
so often,
or the bridge club decided to play
so frequently.
It's not my fault the job is so demanding.
or
the schedule ended up like it is.
We may not choose a situation
but we **do** choose
what we do with it.
It is our choice how we
respond to it.
It is our choice what we make
or allow to be
or communicate as
most important.

Nor does it make much of a dent to say
"It's all for you."
Seldom home,
working all the time,
involved in countless charitable projects
"all for you."
But what the other,
or others,
may well want
is **not** all the things money can buy,
but presence,

the presence of the one they
love.
It may well be that,
no matter how often a person says
"It's all for you,"
what the other really hears is that—
whatever it is that takes that person away—
is far more important.

Number one priority,
leaning,
setting the other free—
all these can be communicated in
countless ways.
No relationship is exactly the same as another;
therefore the symbols used in communication
are never the same.
What is an absolutely essential symbol
to one relationship
may not be to another.
But the inescapable truth is that
however it's said and lived,
however it is communicated,
a person is aware of being "number one"
or special
to another.
He or she
knows it.
And when that person **isn't** "number one"
or special,
he or she knows that, too.

A Feeling of Specialness

Specialness
is **the attitude of tender respect
extended to another,**
an attitude that says
"You are unique and precious to me."

People love in a lot of ways.
Symbols differ.
The manner of exchanging
love symbols
may differ greatly.
For some,
dressing up and going out
is vital to the maintenance of the
relationship.
For others, it is as foreign as Mars.
Some relationships thrive on
gentle teasing;
others don't.
Some are filled with gifts of
flowers, cards, notes or
poems;
others count on
jokes, fish fries and ball games.
The music of some

genuine relationships is
classical,
of others
—just as real—
country western.
Some relationships are comfortable
in jeans and tank tops,
others in evening gowns and suits.
Some couples ride in jeeps and pick-up trucks,
others in limousines.
Some go to the opera, others to
drive-in movies.
Some indeed may include all of the above
at different moments.
But no matter what the
manifestation,
how it is expressed,
if it is genuine,
if there is real love
between two persons,
if each is standing even stronger and straighter
in individuality,
there is always the nebulous but
very real element of
specialness, each to the other.
The two involved know
beyond doubt
that they are special to one another.
Each knows he or she is
precious
in the heart and sight of the other.
On this point of regarding each other as

precious
or special,
we can be very careless.
Under the guise of
"We have been married too long,"
or
"He (or she) knows; I don't have to break my
back proving it,"
or
"We are beyond that stage,"
it is very easy to let
preciousness tarnish,
to allow specialness to disintegrate.
We may be communicating
to the other an attitude of
disinterest that says
"You or another—
it really doesn't matter."
Here comes the elephant,
snorting and blowing,
grudgingly accepted,
living in the front room.
We can say what we will about it:
"It really doesn't matter,"
or
"The little things don't count,"
but they do.
Lacking the mutual regard of
specialness,
all that is left is the waif-feeling and
the empty fountains and
the ticking time bombs.

Specialness, however,
is an imponderable.
It is not concrete and is even less able
to be expressed in any kind of
percentage
than honesty or trust.
If trust has been broken,
dishonesty slipped into,
situations can be named,
incidents brought up,
events remembered.
Specialness,
the quality of being precious to another,
or regarding another in
a special way,
is more elusive than that.
It has to do with the kind of care
often present
at a time of birth or death,
at a time of tragedy or
serious sickness.
At those times a special light
burns in the hearts and faces
of those present.
There is a glow,
the glow of concern and caring
for someone precious.
Signs of affection abound.
Extra phone calls,
just to see how the loved one is doing,
become automatic.
The tone of voice drops

the harshness often dissipates.
There is not so much coldness or
insensitivity.
A hand
seldom grasped
now reaches out to hold
and be held.
Communication is happening.
The message:
You are special to me,
you are precious.
My world is not the same without you.
In fact
I dare not even think of my life
apart from you.
I may not know well
how to say it,
show it,
I am not a poet or a troubadour,
but my heart is trying to tell you
you are precious.
Seldom
is the message not heard.
The main key to
communicating preciousness
is not to be a poet or a troubadour
but to
want to communicate it.
And you can only want to
if it is true.
What is tragic
is that

it often is true
but it doesn't get said.
We wait,
thinking it unimportant,
trivial,
not "my style"—
wait
until it is too late for one reason
or another.
The train has pulled out
and left us behind.

Every genuine loving relationship
has that about it which breathes
specialness and preciousness.
These attitudes automatically give birth to
respect and beauty.
These, too, are
imponderables,
scarcely—if at all—able to be
measured, weighed, evaluated.
But there is no problem in
recognizing when they are
present,
or in feeling the hurt when they are
absent.

Respect—
like the bald eagle—
is endangered.
For many reasons,
partly social,

partly economic,
partly based on personal experiences,
we hardly know what respect is.
We are taught so much to
use
things,
use them and
when they are worn out or
no longer useful
to throw them away and
get new ones.
Some of the world around us is indeed to be
used
but much of it is to be met.
Not used.
They are not the same.

In order to "meet"
a segment of the world,
whether it be
human or not,
we must have an attitude of
quiet receptivity,
We must be able and want to
listen.
We must desire not to possess
or capture,
but to allow ourselves to be
captured by it;
we must not want so much
to wrap it up and
take it home

as to ask it—
be it music, art, poetry
or a human relationship—
to allow us to merge with it,
to touch us,
to accept us as guest and partner.

Notice in any art museum—
any that has truly fine art.
Before each of the best pieces there is a bench.
Some think it is just a place to rest.
A place to sit down between
looking at pictures or statues.
Not so.
Sensitive viewing of art requires
proper distance.
From too close a vantage,
the magic of the
masterpiece is lost;
the whole is lost in too close a scrutiny
of the parts.
From too far away,
again
the masterpiece is lost,
for we cannot see
well enough
the harmonious interraction of
the parts making the whole.
The benches are not
randomly set,
much less are they just resting places.
They are purposely placed at the

proper distance
from the work in front of it
so we can see it
from the best distance and angle,
look at it reverently,
hear and understand its message.
Nothing can be heard or seen
without respect,
without proper distance.
There is no art greater,
more God-like
more healing,
more important than
the art of building, maintaining and
fostering loving relationships.
Though the symbols and
manner of expression may vary,

the needs for respect,
quiet, specialness and
preciousness
are essential.

Johnny is a young man,
a Greek-god young man,
who loves motorcycle racing.
It is a rough, dirty sport.
When it rains, mud and slush
are thrown around by the bucketload.
In summer's roasting heat, bikes and riders
take a terrible beating.
People become passionately involved
in this sport.
They care.
Between races, Johnny always
props his bike up,
takes out a rag and cleaning fluid,
focuses his mind and
lovingly tends to his bike.
As much dirt and dust as possible
are rubbed off.
Parts are oiled,
filters cleaned,
nuts and bolts tightened.
Were the bike a human being,
it would surely
know beyond doubt that
it is loved.
Often things like
motorbikes,

rare coins, stamps, flowers
and animal pets of all kinds—
were they able to know—
would know heart-deep how they are
loved, respected, cared for,
while
countless persons could not even guess
anyone would miss them if they
died on the street.
It is indeed a strange thing to
ponder
how people who can
expend such love and special regard for
all sorts of inanimate and living things
find it simply impossible to express the same
gentle concern for another human being.
Hours can be whiled away
cleaning and oiling a favorite
rifle,
but scarcely a moment spent
fondly caressing the face
of a beloved.
It is killing to be
second place
to a rifle,
or a bankbook
or a snowmobile
or anything else.

Respect and regard for preciousness and
attitudes that bloom like flowers
whenever beauty is seen.

But then beauty is never just seen—
beauty is always entered into.
As the symbols of love differ,
one person's beauty is not
necessarily another's.
I know a man who could dream of
little more beautiful
than the boxing skill of
Sugar Ray Robinson.
It was ballet, poetry and the primal excitement
of the battle and hunt—
all rolled into one.
Someone else might see only
brutality there.

The point is that when
whatever or whoever presents beauty to us—
beauty which we grasp and allow to grasp us—
feelings of preciousness and respect
rise immediately in our hearts.
A fierce desire grows
to protect and preserve,
to enhance and allow life.
We feel the dual sensations of
pride and humility—
great pride,
for in the face of beauty we always
are proud;
humility,
because in the face of great beauty
we always
seem so small,
so honored to be there.

We find delicious,
exciting beauty in
polished wood,
fast horses,
delicate flowers,
masterful craftsmanship on
dishes, guns, iron work,
in the writing of a poem or the painting of a
picture.
Because we find beauty there,
our attitude changes;
manners soften,
our spirits deepen
In the presence of a
celebrity
we find beautiful or powerful,
we can scarcely find our tongues.
We stammer and stutter,
perhaps
make no sense at all.
The celebrity
knows we are impressed,
knows he or she is
something special
in our lives,
knows what power
he or she exerts over us.

But does not all love make of
those involved
celebrities?
Can there ever be love

without the sense of
beauty,
giving rise in its discovery
to feelings of specialness,
preciousness and respect.
True,
living close to the celebrity may
erode that person's beauty in our eyes,
but
if that were to happen,
then the power would be gone,
the specialness erased.
That person would just be
ordinary then,
like everyone else,
no one special.
When that happens within a relationship
called love,
when there is nothing special left, when
there is no respect or regard for preciousness,
the poles fall over,
the rope lies on the ground.
The fountain dries up.

There may well not be
more important words
in a relationship than
"please" and "thank you."
We can say,
"I love you,"
when we have to,
but if we have not also said all along
"please" and "thank you,"

how much can love
be believed?
When a person asks,
"please,"
it acknowledges the need to ask,
not demand.
It admits that the relationship—
the togetherness with another—
is a gift, not a right.
One tells the other,
"I come as a poet, not a pirate,
I ask to be let in,
I seek permission to enter."
Then "please"
becomes a sweetness stronger than force,
a binding tighter than chains.
It is a word of a guest,
not a crusader.
"Please" says,
"I know you don't have to,
but I hope you will."
"Please"
is a word used in the face
of beauty,
of specialness and preciousness.
Its absence clearly says,
"I find no beauty here,
nothing special."
Courtesy, politeness, manners—
no matter how crude or unpolished—
always,
invariably

accompany a sense
of encountering the beautiful.
And if a beloved is not beautiful,
can they be beloved?

"Thank you"
indicates that a gift was given
and recognized as a gift.
It was not a
debt repaid,
a right rendered,
a law fulfilled.
Gifts
are more than that.
Gifts can only be gifts
when freely given.
But what was merely a
right rendered
can bloom into a beautiful gift
when met with a "thank you."
Not just a surface sign of
social compliance,
but a genuine "thank you"
from the spirit,
acknowledging our poverty,
our inability to
be the same or do as well
without the gift of the other.
"Please" and
"thank you"
state clearly who the other is,
what the other means

in a loving relationship.
They say volumes about the other's degree
of specialness and preciousness
in our eyes,
about the
appreciation of beauty,
the awareness of the quality of giving
involved in all relationships.
Love
is a necessity.
For health, sanity and safety,
we need to know we are special,
precious,
beautiful in the sight of those who
love us.
Were we all to know that,
to feel that,
we would see in marvelous quantities
the visages of demons change before our eyes
into the lovely faces of angels.

The Angel and The Demon

Love
and also the lack of love
are powers.
As with all powers, love is
neutral.

Power itself is neither good nor bad,
creative nor destructive.
The outcome of power,
its effects on our lives and world,
depends on other factors.
Consistently throughout these pages,
we have stated our main premise:
Love is not a luxury—
it is a necessity.
The power
within each of us—
reaching, raging, rushing
to find its connection—
wears the face of the
angel
if integrated into a loving relationship.
If not,
it wears the

multitudinous face of the demon.
What is most helpful to understand,
as with the model of love
as a relationship,
is that the need for love
and loving relationships
is power.

Power
is either an angel or a demon
depending on what we do with it,
on how well we handle it.

The truth about power
is that, again,
it is like a rope
having two ends.
We might call either end of this
rope of power
the angel and the demon.
Looking at this model of the
rope, however,
it becomes obvious
they are not two different things—
they are but different ends of the
same rope.
It is not possible to
cut off one end of a rope!
What must be done is
that the whole rope
must be placed in a context where it will be
beneficial to everyone.

The difference between a Hitler and a
St. Francis
was not simply that one was bad and one good,
one a Saint and one a killer—
the fundamental difference was that
both had immense power,
yet
one integrated that power into a whole,
healthy personality;
the other
allowed the power to become uncontrolled.
Hitler no longer possessed the power,
the power possessed him.
The famous thinker Rainer Maria Rilke
put it simply,
if you kill my demon,
you also kill my angel.
If you put out the fire,
true,
no one can burn down the world,
but neither can the fire light the darkness
or warm the chill off a freezing night.

The question we face
as individuals and as a society
is not simply how to kill
all those elements that so militate against
love and loving relationships.
The demon cannot be killed
any more than one end of a rope
can be cut off.
The quest is not one of killing,

but of integrating the power,
of channeling it,
so that the form of the angel appears
rather than the gargoyle shape of the
demon.
Anyone who reads these pages thoughtfully,
using them as mirrors and as
check lists for the direction of that
vital element,
love
in our lives,
no doubt will find room for growth.
These pages were written in the light
of the ideal,
the goal to be strived for,
the growth to work toward.
There is no such thing as perfect love
or perfect loving relationships,
because
there is no such thing as a perfect human being.
People
are
flawed.
We cannot be perfect;
we can only work at progress.

Whatever these pages lead us to,
personally or relationally,
as areas for growth, we can face them and say,
"I'm going to destroy
the fear, selfishness, apathy
that drains the fountain and saddens

my world with waif-like feelings."
But the demon can only die if
the angel becomes stronger.

It is one thing to say,
"I will be less afraid,"
it is another to say,
"I will allow someone to walk with me
in my fear."
It is one thing to say,
"I will be less self-centered,"
it is another to say,
"If I allow my fountain to be filled
more often,
I will have much more energy and willingness
to fill the fountain of another."
It is trying only to kill the demon
without recognizing the true nature of power
to say,
"I will stop nagging,"
without also saying,
"I will allow myself to be held."
Only people who feel good
about themselves
can be part of a loving relationship.
That gift of
improving self-image is
partly a gift to ourselves
which we acquire
by putting ourselves in the way of it,
recognizing its importance.
But it is also a gift

we must give to others.
Each is a mirror
before which the other stands.
If all one sees reflected back is an inadequate,
stumbling, not-good-enough partner,
then what else can the other do but agree?
And thus agreeing,
there is nothing else to give the other.
The mirrors become so distorted
they are incapable of mirroring back
the beauty that is truly there.

Making love work however
does not depend simply on
killing the demon.
It is not so much a matter of fasting
and doing penance
as it is a matter of feasting
on the God-like qualities others
can offer to us.
We have such a tendency for seeing the world
shallowly,
as divided into opposites,
good and bad,
right and wrong,
night and day,
beautiful and ugly.
Beneath the surface, however,
these opposites are related,
affecting one another,
flowing back and forth.
Little progress can be made if only
one is seen.

Dr. Rollo May
has done extensive work on this question of
the angel and the demon.
He uses the term
"demoniac,"
which is a Greek word
translated into English
as "genius."
"Genius" is the strange
peculiar, mysterious
power emanating out of certain people we call
geniuses,
those who have special communication with
their own inner selves and thus
with the gods.
Regardless of what all else
genius may be,
it is power,
inner power seeking a release,
seeking to express itself.
When this genius is present
along with the talents of a Rembrandt,
Michelangelo or Einstein,

the results are visible and profound.
To a lesser, but not
less important degree,
(at least for us)
the same process of genius seeking release
is unfolding in each of us.
For someone to reach out
respectfully, lovingly
and take the hand of a beloved—
just to hold for a moment—
might—
for that person—
be as great a release of personal,
inner power as Raphael found
in painting his Madonnas.
That gesture may be
as much an expression
of who the person is
and is becoming as any work of a great
master.
That same power, however,
if not integrated in a loving way,
if not involved in a creative kind of release,
can also guide the hand that in anger
strikes the children, breaks the furniture, or
runs the car off the road.
The question is not one of
who is good and who is
evil,
it is fundamentally a question of
how individual power is being channeled.

Dr. May explains with dramatic and
greatly helpful insight that
what we are talking about here is
demonic possession.
Not as in **The Exorcist**,
but whenever an emotion
such as anger, fear, resentment, jealousy
runs out of control,
paralyzing our lives and
becoming the sole concern of consciousness.
Then there is a type of possession in process,
one that must be dealt with or
exorcised.
He uses the context of a
primitive exorcism among jungle tribes.
The external situation
is different from our own,
but the inner dynamics are not.
He recounts the tale of a man
possessed by hatred and resentment,
in a country that occupied his land.
The possession had come to
dominate his life.
The rite of exorcism followed these steps:
  1) The man came to admit the obsession.
  2) He "embraced" the possessing demon by
     putting on a uniform of the hated enemy.
     Thus,
     he "wore" the demon that possessed him.
  3) In the company of the rest of the tribe,
     he acted out his hatred.
He danced,

sang,
threw himself around.
All through the ritual, his clan,
his friends,
were there to support him, to comfort him
and urge him to continue until the
demon was integrated,
replaced by the angel of
tolerance.

Another incident Dr. May tells about
had to do with a man's hatred for his
mother.
She had dominated him totally,
ruined his life
up to the present.
The man desperately wanted to be free of
the possession.

The same steps followed.
   1) He first of all admitted the possession.
   2) He put on the dress of his mother.
   3) He underwent the same ritual,
      wrestling with the demon
      in the company of the tribe—
      always in the company of the tribe.

Dr. May
states very clearly that this would be
impossible to undertake alone.
Our demons are too terrifying
to confront alone.

Exorcism must always be carried out
in the presence of supporting people.

As bizarre as these events may seem,
the dynamics remain constant in our own time.
There can be no escape,
no exorcism,
from the demons of fear, hatred, resentment
without first of all naming what is in control.
There can be no healing or
deepening of love
and loving relationships without first of all
being willing to see where things are,
to answer a check list of some kind,
to peer into a mirror.
When the truth is seen,
a decision is made—
always.
Will I admit and deal with the
overweight problem,
the drinking problem,
the loneliness problem?
Will I embrace it,
face it,
put it on
as a uniform or dress?
Will I wear it,
grasp it from the inside out?
Or
will I deny it?
As a patient who is dying may,
until the end,

deny the stage of the disease
which is robbing him
of life.
The denial may indeed take place,
but it changes nothing
about the dying.
If the decision is to
embrace the
offending demon,
this, too, must be done
in the company of a community—
friends,
family.
And then comes the wrestling,
the turning this way and that,
the running and hiding only
to
face it again and return to the arena.

Earlier we spoke of a
treatment center scene—
where forty or fifty people gathered together
to wrestle with demons,
to transform demons into angels,
to learn to love.
There an angel-filled man spoke the
words of truth and life,
"The only hope for all of us is to
learn to love."
Those may well sound merely like
pretty words,
poetical words and thoughts,

devoid of the stuff of harsh reality.
Those familiar with
redemption and treatment
know such is not the case.
For many in that room,
the angel will be too fearful,
the support too weak,
the skills too fragile.
The truth will not be
faced,
the struggle not undertaken,
the exorcism not finished.
The demons of wall-building, fear, apathy and
dishonesty
will not be transformed into the
angels of
vulnerability, trust, enthusiasm and
gentleness.

But for others
whose time is right
whose time is now,
the slow passage will begin to take place.
Something so real
it defies words will begin to happen
deep within the temple of self;
there will be **a shifting**.
That which was thought
indispensible
for survival will be discarded.
Huge pillars will begin to be moved.

Faintly at first,
then with more and more clarity,
like a sunrise,
there will be the daring to think,
to hope,
to invite;
something really can be different this time,
it can be better.

Self
begins to glow like an electrified orb,
like the brilliant sun,
and in that glowing,
the other in the relationship
wakes to life as well.
One glowing
initiates a response on the part of the
other.
Deep calls unto deep.
The call
is heard and answered.
Poles straighten;
the rope of relationship stretches
in creative tension.
An intricate switch opens
new tracks;
a new way becomes accessible to travel,
ugliness is exchanged for beauty,
the fountain fills.
The waif,
so long familiar,

passes from cold into
Eden-like warmth of specialness.
A miracle has happened,
the world is better, much better,
for this one magical, marvelous event:
that which was lost has been
found.

About the Author

Earnie Larsen's contributions as son, brother, friend, minister, writer, speaker and counselor have long been recognized. He is involved in establishing his own holistic counseling institute, and pioneering work on "Stage II" recovery — getting the most from being human.

Perhaps because of his impressive track record in youth work, chemical dependency counseling and the authorship of more than two dozen books, Earnie is rumored to ride a white horse and eat nails for breakfast. His friends at the pie shop know better.

In this book, as in **Good Old Plastic Jesus,** his best seller, Earnie continues to write about the extraordinary spiritual dimension of ordinary human beings.

Other good books and pamphlets from CompCare Publications

. . . But I Didn't Make Any Noise About It, Cindy Lewis-Steere. A mother's story of her teenage son's drug dependency. This moving account of a family's crisis and painful growth illustrates clearly that as the entire family is affected by one member's drug problem, all members are involved in the recovery process. Recommended by counselors for use in parent and family groups, as well as by individual families. ISBN 0-89638-043-2, pamphlet.

Compulsive Overeater, Bill B. An interpretation of the Twelve Steps of Alcoholics Anonymous (AA) especially for compulsive overeaters. Many thousands of overeaters have heard Bill B. share the way he works the Program and has maintained a seventy-five-pound weight loss for over ten years. Explores each Step, as well as "abstinence," trust, sponsorship, relationships, money, self-inventories, and how all aspects of life interlock. Back to press four times in the first year after publication. ISBN 0-89638-046-7, hard cover.

Consider the Alternative, Lee M. Silverstein. A caring counselor and nationally known lecturer at alcoholism and health conferences has synthesized popular theories about therapy into a personal guide for living. Greeted with enthusiasm by Albert Ellis, Sidney B. Simon (who wrote the foreword), Joel Fort, William Glasser, John Powell, and many other experts. ISBN 0-89638-004-1, paperback.

A Day at a Time. Now with 250,000 in print, this pocket-sized book of daily messages offers confidence, strength, resolve, hope, and serenity. Especially helpful to those in any kind of Twelve Step Program. ISBN 0-89638-000-9, hard cover.

Going Home, *A Re-entry Guide for the Newly Sober,* Janet Geringer Woititz, Ed.D. A compassionate, straight-talking guide for anyone who is newly sober, whether sobriety began in a residential or outpatient program or through AA alone. Examines predicaments, issues, special problems and hurdles faced when a person begins a chemical-free life. By a college professor, alcoholism counselor, and author of *Marriage on the Rocks.* ISBN 0-89638-049-1, pamphlet.

Help for Ourselves, Rick Weber, illustrated by Sam Wilson. An Indian counselor/educator and an Indian artist teamed with members of the Umatilla tribe to produce this brilliantly illustrated version of the Twelve Steps especially for Native Americans. Used as a recovery tool by alcohol- and drug-dependent Native Americans in many United States and Canadian treatment programs. ISBN 0-89638-075-0, pamphlet.

If Only My Family Understood Me . . . Don Wegscheider, foreword by Virginia Satir. A family can find new balance through stress. The same insights which help troubled families can help any family (troubled or not) have more fun living together. A "whole person" approach, particularly useful for alcoholic families and their counselors. ISBN 0-89638-038-6, paperback.

If Only My Wife Could Drink Like a Lady, Jack Nero. Intimate, heartening story of a one-in-ten marriage to survive a wife's alcoholism — by her "mirror alcoholic" husband. Essential information about AA and Al-Anon for alcoholics and those close to them. "May save some lives and ease the tension for families of alcoholics." Jan Frazer Book Review. ISBN 0-89638-052-1, paperback; ISBN 0-89638-057-2, hard cover.

I'm Black & I'm Sober, Chaney Allen. In this first autobiography by a black woman recovering alcoholic, a minister's daughter relives her long struggle with alcoholism. "Deeply dramatic, told in a raw and moving style with humor, anguish, fury, and, finally, hope." *Los Angeles Times.* ISBN 0-89638-008-4, paperback.

I Never Saw the Sun Rise, Joan Donlan. A high school counselor says: "This book should be required reading for every high school student in the country — and for all parents." A true, as-it-happened journal by a talented 15-year-old tells of her drug/alcohol dependency, her treatment, and her recovery. Important insights for teens and adults. ISBN 0-89638-007-6, paperback.

Just So It's Healthy, Lucy Barry Robe. Revised Edition. Foreword by Stanley E. Gitlow, M.D. Drinking and drugs can harm your unborn baby. Up-to-date medical facts about Fetal Alcohol Syndrome (FAS) and effects of other drugs, including often-prescribed and over-the-counter drugs, on unborn infants. Essential information for women and health professionals. ISBN 0-89638-062-9, paperback.

Kids and Drinking, Anne Snyder. Informative, hopeful book for grade school ages is based on experiences of three child alcoholics who began drinking at ages 8, 9, and 11. Excellent discussion focus for children and their parents, teachers, counselors. A youth-alcoholism prevention tool by an award-winning author. ISBN 0-89638-010-6, illustrated paperback.

Life Is Good-bye/Life Is Hello, Alla Bozarth-Campbell, Ph.D. An Episcopal priest and therapist shows how to grieve well through all kinds of loss. She guides a hurting person through the process of grief, whether brought about by physical death, pregnancy, geographic changes and partings, chemical dependency, the death of a dream, or any other of life's jolts. Invaluable for professionals and programs dealing with illness, divorce, death. ISBN 0-89638-061-0, paperback; ISBN 0-89638-060-2, hard cover. Available June '82.

Stepping Lightly, Cynthia Lewis-Steere, illustrations by Diane Baldinger Westby. An A to Z guide for stepparents . . . humor helps blended families survive. A light-hearted look at developing stepparenting skills offers help from the perspective of humor to the forty-three million in this country struggling to build or just to survive in blended families. Includes a guide for starting a stepparents support group and a workbook for recording, in a year's worth of weekly entries, the progress of a blend. ISBN 0-89638-051-3, paperback.

Survival Kit, Susan B. Anthony, Ph.D. Triumph over suffering, break through to serenity with these lifesaving tools. The author, a counselor, lecturer, leader in the alcoholism field, is the grandniece and namesake of one of America's best known women. In this inspirational book, back in print by popular demand, she shares the tools she and other "survivors" have found to overcome suffering in their lives. ISBN 0-89638-050-5, paperback.

This Will Drive You Sane, Bill L. Little. Foreword by Albert Ellis. Excerpted by *Reader's Digest.* "A droll, paradoxical look at problem-solving in everyday life. Enlightening and funny, it will dare you to cling to neurotic symptoms." *The Book Report.* Shawnee, Oklahoma. ISBN 0-89638-047-5, paperback.

144

The Twelve Steps for Everyone . . . who really wants them. Keys to spiritual health and emotional wealth based on the Twelve Step path developed by AA. Clearly interpreted by members of EHA (Emotional Health Anonymous). ISBN 0-89638-013-0, paperback.

The Winner's Way, A Beginner's Guide to the Twelve Steps, Carol Hegarty. Introduces a Program newcomer to these all-important, effective concepts in language anyone can understand and relate to. Answers basic questions about the Steps and includes a glossary of Program terms. A cornerstone for treatment programs and an aid to Twelve Step people everywhere. ISBN 0-89638-053-X, pamphlet.

Young Alcoholics, Tom Alibrandi. An alcoholism counselor takes a hard look at teenage drinking. "Offers young problem drinkers (and parents who want to help them) practical, proven series of approaches to recovery." *Los Angeles Times.* ISBN 0-89638-014-9, paperback.

All of the above books are published by and available from CompCare Publications. None is either endorsed or opposed by the author of this book. Ask us to send you a free CompCare Publications catalog of quality books and other materials emphasizing a positive approach to life's problems for young people and adults on a broad range of topics. If you have questions, call us toll free at 800/328-3330. (Minnesota residents: Call 612/559-4800.)

CompCare ®
publications

2415 Annapolis Lane, Minneapolis, Minnesota 55441
a division of Comprehensive Care Corporation